Old and New Schools

by Maryellen Gregoire

Nancy E. Harris, M.Ed—Reading
National Reading Consultant

capstone
classroom
Heinemann Raintree • Red Brick Learning
division of Capstone

I see teachers.

I see students.

I see lunch boxes.

THE BOYS' BRIGADE
THE BOYS' BRIGADE
THE BOYS' BRIGADE

I see flags.

Do unto others as you would have them do unto you

I see teachers.

I see students.

I see lunch boxes.

I see flags.